Kingdom

Myronn Hardy

New Issues Poetry & Prose

A Green Rose Book

New Issues Poetry & Prose
The College of Arts and Sciences
Western Michigan University
Kalamazoo, Michigan 49008

First Edition, 2015.

ISBN: 978-1-936970-35-3 (paperbound)

Library of Congress Cataloging-in-Publication Data:
Hardy, Myronn.
Kingdom/Myronn Hardy
Library of Congress Control Number: 2014952971

Editor: William Olsen
Managing Editor: Kimberly Kolbe
Layout Editor: McKenzie Lynn Tozan
Assistant Editor: Alyssa Jewell
Art Direction: Nicholas Kuder
Design: Nate Whittington
Production: Paul Sizer
                     The Design Center, Frostic School of Art
                     College of Fine Arts
                     Western Michigan University
Printing: McNaughton & Gunn, Inc.

Kingdom

Myronn Hardy

New Issues

WESTERN MICHIGAN UNIVERSITY

Also by Myronn Hardy

Approaching the Center
The Headless Saints
Catastrophic Bliss

For Houssam   Yassine

I've listened.

Contents

We are taken in wheelbarrows.

But you hear the sea suddenly.

We should dream a little. In fact, do more than dream.

—Mohamed Choukri

The coming of daylight made him anxious and unhappy.

—Paul Bowles

One sheep foresees a flood   tawny
    water scalloped.

Kingdom

The poplars have no leaves.
Like femurs in ground   nothing
but air to kick or imagine kicking if they
were attached to joint   tibia.

We decide to wander.
This day   a star's false
omnipotence
prismed through sky.

How it radiates over everything.
When younger   you caught crayfish in
that tributary. In a pot   boiled at home   everything
smelled of clay   sediment   the drowned.

The oaks   common in these woods.
Unfortunately   we are not   the way we
think   the way we'd lead   if.
But they would cannon   rifle or we'd

be ominously missing. The desert
drying us to zinc   iron. But the
Barbary lions would be brought back
from extinction to roar our names   others.

Hunters holding bows   arrows
withering to thread. That lake's version
of green is where you swam   your swimming
pool in summer   the splashing.

How water cascades   those watching
unaware of pulverized rock   smooth
but compromised. Those on the backs
of donkeys are happiest. Saddles with

bells   chlorophylls patterns keeping away
evil eye but where is that?
Can it be seen? Is it truly a look
of someone with a different power?

We find the bleached jaw of a donkey
beneath an oak whose bark is splotched
with moss. It seems more boomerang than
what it is. Perhaps it always comes back?

This ground where leaves have
broken to net will break into something
smaller   particles   atoms   until nothing.
Is this what we become or is it shadow?

The dark on ground   on trunks   that
realm of utter unobtrusiveness. So unlike
the artificial florescence of orange soda.
A chemical in a lab made to trick.

Restrained colors of these woods
until   at that table   the plastic
bottle   siren. *Take a picture
of me on something fallen.*

That bare trunk that slopes over
stagnant river. Gnats   winged particles
over reflecting boughs.
The radishes grown here are sweet

as is the wheat harvested one week ago.
This is a secret   you tell me. So many
secrets in towns. The sheep eat what is left.
We watch them follow each other.

The shepherd's orange shoes match
the soda on that eroding table. The picnic
the boys are preparing there   chops dusted
with cumin   ginger grilling.

Are the sheep aware of this? The shepherd
young   was he told why he guides them?
Why they eat green-wild things   the tops of white
radishes   green stems scattered after harvest?

Then to that green roof   that holy house.
The man the villagers admire decades after death.
That place is for him. Those seeking shelter
after such distance   everything threadbare.

How quiet it has become   brown doves   the coos
they make as calm as rugs drying on pumice walls.
Two old men talk about the kingdom.
How it has changed yet they haven't

other than hair   muscle   the way
they sleep. The young in various
twists   tumultuous acts among trees   starlings.
The two old men are copper in that village.

They watch swatches of smoke kink
from chimneys   the roofs where corn dries.
We want to be pious.
We want to give up all that is not.

Yet you couldn't live in that village.
Yours slightly larger   a café with pastries
beneath glass. A woman bundles brushwood to back.
She could be my grandmother   great grandmother.

Spine like sycamore   her
sons practicing something
they have been taught.
The call   again.

The stir of day as we ride to the town
where we began.
A feast in a restaurant
where music is electronic.

I will build a house in the woods.
Build it near the lake where trout
jump out of boredom.
There I will die among poplars   oaks.

We wash our hands.

Blue Cards in the Café of Old Men

Yassine plays cards with old men.
They see him as a son who remained
in a town the young flee because they have to.
There is a cloud in the café   brown as bark
yet no storm above them. Only the dark
darkening that room of smoke.

The cards have blue backs   lines of smoke
spinning from imaginary airplanes where those men
are pilots   their cards on the floor suddenly dark.
Yassine wants them to ascend   wants to have remained
a magic trick his father performed against bark
where he disappeared. He wants to

leave that town but doesn't want to
disappoint those old men who smoke
themselves to clouds surrounding oak bark
as if gauze. They are wounded men.
We are an arena of limestone which has remained
despite time. Heads split   arms dropped with age dark

with rust veins like earth itself   deeper the dark
dazzles. Outside women are kneading   oiling dough to
fry against seasoned steel. They have remained
constant in that town   feeding that town as smoke
rises from steel   from warm bread those men
eat playing cards from day to sunset   skin slowly to bark.

This is seen through a smudged window where the bark
of oaks is mossy against the café. The curtains are dark
with filth   regret feral yet caged. The men
collect cards   stare at cards in fans   want Yassine to
disappoint them. Want Yassine to peel smoke
away from skin   to run   to have remained

the boy his father left. To have remained
the boy in love with bark.
The cloud in the café is still brown smoke
making them sick. They cough in the dark
they have created to
cope with the boy they've ruined. Those men

have remained magnificently dark
like the bark which hasn't greened to
moss. Yassine will blink   smoke among old men.

Sheep: Flood Foreseen

—for Lucille Clifton

Sheep tear into clover. Teeth speckled

green   tongues muddy with minerals.

Their necks like boughs that grew

too thick   almost albino from

torsos   gaudy   greedy   a coup that failed.

One sheep foresees a flood   tawny water scalloped.

The wind with its angular currents folds

through an oak forest. Wet legs are umber

yet the rest cream   coarse.

The shepherd is writing a book

he doesn't understand.

His language has almost drowned

but he continues struggling with breath.

This is my life   the meaning of my life.

Apertures

There is a pink house on the green.
Like some giant azalea pruned
into a stack of boxes.
The monkeys inside escape   chase
cherries they somehow remember

from a village where girls knotted lace
about auburn tails   fur matted.
Their lives   a schematic of apertures.
They can't read   neither
mothers   grandmothers.

The men have left for a city spelled
out in a common alphabet.
They will return with women   mute
yet pens never leave hands.
Their goat-skinned pads dampen

with poems yet lips   more like
latches   pink as that house.

Silver

The boy kicks the ball to his sister
on the steps of the church where
fruit skins rot. They both see

through glasses as their father warns
them to be gentle. The ball rolls to me
like a line of a poem when the window

is up   the air of morning   juniper.
I let the ball roll until their mouths
sag to one side.

How could he not play with us?
Meany-meany.
I kick as if Belhanda.

The ball spins between feet.
The boy laughs   kicks   his taller
sister runs around us   sees grass.

The church   a giant bell   blemished.
Its ring turns her hands   ears silver.
Her brother hits the ball with forehead.

Silver shines.
A silver syllable about her neck.
Silver saliva on teeth.

Silver subverts her playing.
Silver slides from mouth.
Silver more somber now.

Silver moths shimmer.
Silver dust swats grass.
Silver slaps her brother's head.

Silver slows
the sloping   the sphere   the surge
on silver land.

Silver coins without surrender.
Meany-meany   who is mean?
Who wants it all to fall?

The crumbling in pupils   dissent
to subdue integrity.
Who hears the chiming?

What You've Been Given

They have given you the name Obama
even though it isn't yours.
The woman slicing cake behind
the counter   her son wheeling through
the market loud when he sees you inside
yourself: *Who is there?*
What world do you see? I want to see.
In the medina   a man offers water   the jug's
top blotted with tar. He puts on a jellaba
as it is six. *I am Stevie Wonder*   he says
pressing shades over eyes. He points his eyes
to clouds   rocks head from side to side.
His son plays a stringed instrument
until his fingers are numb.
What is the use of feeling without ardor?
The day to day of it   the woman slicing
cake behind the counter.
You know his son   stand beside him near
a loam wall. Straining horses pass
with scarred skin. When they sleep
standing   they are among fruit trees.
Craning necks to bite through white cores.
Crisp   fresh   the sound of surrender.
Obama   let Stevie Wonder take
a picture with Obama.

Gigou

The cedar forest is soporific.
Needles more azure than ecru   air
of a wood oddly ancient yet we are not.
Contained in a moment contemporary   ours

are short lives   the expectation
of the car engine that pops   stalls.
The land quickly arid   rock cluttered
appearing more like ruins of a people

obsessed with walls.
How glare is always copper
then sphere   ocher sometimes crimson.
It is a flat house of mud where

sheep are kept. Sheep whose
wool   tawny   faces brown.
In the car you tell me white
is preferred   that Muhammad

relayed this preference on a brown
peninsula where brown blew in currents.
Rachid keeps these sheep   feeds
them rye   red clover   beets.

Waits in a house   dim.
This isn't his mind   his thoughts
like bolts jagged   beautiful
in a sky pitch   clear.

He grinds apples in milk.
Serves this to us in glasses   the room
still dim. Omar has known
him for eight years.

Calls him kind   perhaps
the most   more of a dream
this way. Human   yes
but a dream humans have.

The ideal of us   the perfection
professed but without understanding.
The selflessness you see in Rachid
is more in the sheep he nourishes.

You have selected two.
Pulled them by curled horns
to inspect   to mark for a kill
in November.

The sacrifice they will
become   their necks cut
clean with your knife.
It is time   you tell me.

A tradition where a man sees
life drained red on his hands.
Respect sought quietly
from a father always silent.

The earth red for kilometers
as we leave. The same red
as the frames your cousin
wears   dark lenses shielding

a sun not ready to give up altitude.
In two months sheep will be fatter.
This is why Rachid waits   why he
holds rye in palm   sheep tongues

over palm sometimes
over pulse. Meat
in a house where
hay   manure   sweat

in wool   the scent
pleasant to you yet eyes water.
You sneeze as sun summons
a border we will cross.

Proximity

When I'm old   there will be tea

poured from an aluminum pot.

There will be stories as cards are dealt.

Such comfort among horse chestnuts

like monsters yet gentle   green beings

that protect. The prickly bits of them burst

brown to ground. Thump to tiles   walkways

heads of those who linger. The ground

overwrought with canola where I will

rest among friends   cards bending.

But I am not yet old.

Sitting at tile table eating soup   tearing

baguette to pieces   a train we are both within

yet see long   loud in pieces   connected by steel.

A man my age carries two green pumpkins.

The orange of his mind is imagination itself.

The hum it invents among clatter.

The world is orange.

What We Call Destroyed

It is the flash of egrets from dry reeds.

That destroyed land is the destruction

in us but destruction may be too

harsh   too imprecise for what this is.

For we are both destroyed   saved.

Light does more than flash about us.

The breaking of gray among cork.

The spilling of silver   opaque   wide

as what is unknown. But the wind

is there. Violent in its pursuit

to snap   force most to crumble.

Blow the world into something worth

itself   worth egrets exposing wings

wide   their starry backs during day.

Land of reeds where shepherds

usher flocks. Where we are woven

warm   alive. How the wind

twists reeds to hold itself   baskets

of itself for someone to bear.

Spring Moths

—after Youssef El Khorrib

A green sky is an omen of leaves.
The grandeur of beliefs where

cathedrals are as tall as minarets.
What glides through sky?

What cyclopic beings bend among
sacred protrusions   anemic palms frail

as kingdom   frail as those leaving on boats?
Silent prayer on boats made of paper   wood

slats bruised with corroding nails.
Women watch   wait   worry.

What will water wage?
What will render us silent even though we speak?

Barbed wire across lips   teeth caged   eels
twisting through throats.

The dead are among us.
We reach for them with scarlet hands.

The moon   again.
Its glow is sonic over ocean   the city's

sallow buildings.
It is spring when we explode to moths.

The dust like gunpowder   works of fire
yet nothing burns.

Haze

This blue day exists for us all.
How life is known here   only here.
Staring at sky near sea   sunglasses
keeping glare minimal.

You are some version of Hendrix
on a beach in Essaouira.
The way you live   bound
to philosophy spreading

yet feared. The way some presume
it retreats to a past stilted.
Conflicts needing to be re-resolved.
What is modernity when dogma

impels us to water
where anglerfish light
themselves grotesquely?
At the bottom   everything like this.

But we will smoke in a room without
ventilation. We will hear the tapping
in a northern city. We will cough   laugh
at the world opaque.

A great-grandparent from Damascus
who walked in a desert to Fes.
The sand consistently in throat
minced voice.

If he could   what would this
relative say to you here? His judgment
of you here? You   tall as a short oak.
You hungry   relaxed in this rented room.

Rented to hide
the glory of height   the induced
laughter   the dulling
of brain   cells dilapidated.

The world is a test.
When tempted   what do you do?
There   on sand   women
laugh with us.

Their wet clothes never dry.
Nothing dry in dreams   only
rain   sea   the constant
dripping of everything.

To turn from them is murder.
You see yourself in agony   arrows
through skin   the ribbons
they force into sea.

The haze is horizon   the air itself.
Clarity is gone but was it ever there?
Yes   to you yes. Your ideas   your
philosophy passed onto you by your father.

What now? What after running?

Towers

Everything is gravel beneath his brogues.
That grinding sound promises another step   some distance
among empty   unfinished houses more like shells discarded.

The builders come from a town an hour away with shovels   cement
buckets   bread   oranges. They are as dusty as the moon.
Scorched skin   auburn.

They notice the shoes   the seersucker slacks   the white shirt   the leather
briefcase of the man passing them. *Salaam*   he say   his glasses
shielding eyes with mirrors.

He is from a place that is new.
We want to see towers of glass   know dust as theory
but these clothes don't shed easily   this skin.

What would we do there? Perhaps be hated
as we are here? Looked at   then down.
We disappear.

Regime is our knowledge.

Consider the Dust

Where there are protests   these
streets of stone   soil   you are with me.
This might be imagination   a mind
where drought has given way to illusion.

Perhaps an oil spill over land once
fertile where cashew trees grew profound
with butter. The outrage is justified.
There is no purpose of nation if it doesn't allow

a frame where happiness zigzags teal.
The teal of sky   stones   sea where teal
whales splash teal water because they are teal.
We are wild now.

Pretending not to be for too long.
We burn like stars   falling
stars deftly finding ocean.
Tanks grind streets to powder.

The mad   madder   the throng
unconscious of fear.
You are with me.
This capital be damned.

The anger of gesture   former authorities
mere roads of which to stomp.
Roads of rubble leading
to a freedom without construction.

How are we to know what this is?
Regime is our knowledge.
You are with me among
copper dust   among

the revolt   the revolting beneath
feet in another country rich yet
without the same supremacy.
Can you read the dust?

This horizon   full of it.
It is difficult to breathe
but this feels actual   this feels new.
Our lungs will heal   mere preparation

for air   oxygen that energizes.
Tell those who are afraid to stare
at this sky   this dusty sky
that glitters quartz.

Read this as our lives now.
A code in the desert we have made.

As a Woman Collects Leaves

You stand there   in front of me.
Blood stains your clothes.
You wait for something to show
in my face   something of judgment

but there is nothing there   at least
nothing you can discern.
I am happy to see you
after these months away.

The season pressed into leaves   golden.
What do I know of tradition?
For me   the burden of anything ancient
is weightless   something dissolved

in saltwater   thinned in wind above ships.
The knife to neck inflicts a geyser.
A dark eye dims.
It is over   you say.

I expected more hostility.
The sheep's need to remain.
Its bliss for pasture   electric through veins.
But so calm to ground   the head

pulled back as a woman collects leaves.
What happened to the pain you felt?
That animal's pain   volatile in you.
That gentleness to fur   your hands there.

Perhaps this is your violence,
The kind you refuse to humans   too afraid
to show them   not knowing how to get
away with it   vengeance aloof   scary.

Women burn hair from its face.
Hack its cooked skull in half.
Curled horns sawed   charred.
You pull the kidneys from carcass.

They are two purple jewels
still warm   still shimmering.
You skewer these.
Hold over smoking

alder with the liver.
You and I eat them
with bread before the heart
is salted   dusted with cumin.

My heart beats.
My heart pumps.
My heart is muscle
as is the sheep's in my mouth.

In my mouth   this heart is supple   spiced.
I am the same killer.
The same killer without
custom as a woman collects leaves.

Beat

Your uncle has told you to leave this country.
Fight for yourself   this place no longer worth youth.
You sit with him at a café.
Tea is poured brown.

Chairs against a wide window   you both are silent.
Prison for protest   ideals   the kingdom where merit lifts.
The old king demanded lies   truth only at night   behind
bedroom doors   the language of ecstasy.

A friend passes without seeing you.
He carries a box of walnut pastries for a grandfather
who died that morning   the ribbon curled   choking fingers white.
You see him   the baseball

cap   the sneakers worn with running.
You say nothing.
Watch him walk into light   round a corner
where drums beat from blown speakers.

Lacquer

When chaos ignites after a despot
is forced red   there is a prediction
of freedom. A false simplicity
in town squares where flags
are raised   waved fervently
by those deemed feeble.
Consider cities where flies
take to wounds. Where wounds
are lacquered cups overflowing
with tea   bitter   scalding.
Ahmed has taken to sea cold
as color   brackish as quarry.
How stingrays swim with him   in dark
water sliced suddenly with sun.
Relief   the gun dropped
from hand   water in his hand stings.
Relieved of history   its
infinity plundered.
He is solitary in that water   at least
from those who waged with him.
That morning farmers brought
pomegranates to market.
Men with red teeth weighed fruit
in containers kilo after kilo.
Red seeds blushed skins   a task
to tear away but such taste.
The breaking in mouth   sweet bursts.
The wonder of regime   distant.
The distance of a star yet its
presence covers his face.
The blindness it creates   dazzles.
Cones fray   burst.
The fever he refuses to fight.

Drafting

—for Ahmed Awad

We eat at McDonald's because they
don't exist in Khartoum. It is New Year's
Day yet your father's spine is old.

Surgeons split the bone   plant
seeds in fluid   minerals
dissolve in saline.

Twenty-one days in a city that bruises.
Your hotel room is a lesion   a labyrinth
of faults. I'm silly with English.

Discuss pyramids   exiled
peoples   ask why you
haven't seen the Sphinx.

My father   you say.
The French fries on my tray
turn to spikes. I wish

to pierce my throat but I've
already been dumb.
Mouth open   Pandora's jar.

Ahmed is drafting a tower.
Unlike Babel's   it will not
topple   harm those

below with gravity.
It will be a place to climb   escape
pillage   the fire for being dark.

Yes   this is our tower.
Your father standing
winged at its peak.

Honor

—*for Amina Filali*

It is a felt scarf that unravels from her mouth.
Folds of sunset spilling on a street made of hexagons.

This is the city where Jean Genet is buried.
Where women make cookies to serve at weddings.

What is privacy when there has been invasion?
When all the opal has been taken   the mine given to thieves?

Jean Genet's mother was a prostitute.
Your mother didn't want you to become   to be perceived as one.

Obsessed with honor yet who is honorable?
Take her   this is the agreement.

You have debauched rapture.
Her father in a room mourning   white petals

once water through his fingers.
What is bravery when we are silent?

When we know everyone around us is wrong   our tradition wrong?
Your face on posters shattered as if glass.

Veiled women jutting posters in air.
This daughter   our daughter   not again.

The capital bereft with their marching   their sun-glassed
faces   rats rough about their feet.

The Waiting

I see you as a boy.
I see you standing near your father.

Looking at your father   needing
your father   showing him that need.

This when now you do everything without him.
This when he turns away when you reveal strategy.

This when your friends seek suggestion.
You are a prince in a city without royalty.

A prince in a family where your father isn't king.
You have chosen your grandmother.

You see her facial tattoos as charms   as symbols
of more than marriage   the people here forever.

Her teeth are gold crowns.
In her house there is freedom   continuity unlike your parents'.

Even now you bring her water when she sleeps.
The sea is so far from here but there are lakes   waterfalls.

The sea is near you now.
Its crashing echoes throughout the apartment.

What new music is this?
What is to be learned from it?

The Atlantic once again   perhaps there
is more salt than water.

There are women who wait to be asked inside.
Perhaps they are escaping fathers gone mute.

You have led them to the coast   to your apartment.
The boy you once were still somewhere within water.

This is what those women see.
Particularly what they see in eyes that glisten as if tigers'.

The boy waiting for his father to lay hand to shoulder.
The father who hears of the knife at University.

The father who knows his son left
during mayhem   windows in pieces.

The knife held by a man from Sahara
then used to pierce him hollow.

This because a girl with hidden hair
was pulled too close.

Red flags in the desert   peculiar
red in a russet landscape.

The claim is peace yet they claim
themselves as does another land.

Bandits wait in sunned   forsaken
corners perhaps to disturb idleness.

Tiny groups roam heat   practice
themselves among themselves.

But you don't know this.
Away from the disaster it caused in the capital.

It is the sea.
Your father away from that sea.

He is on land in a house tiny   white   almost invisible.
You wade as he waits inside.

The Treachery of Dream

—after Amine El Khalifi

In the dream   a man is forced to
remove his doomed hat. Stars
captive lose control   the pressure

of atmosphere   twirls to explosion.
Does this dream include me?
The dream I'm having while I sleep   when

I walk in the land of Dixie.
In the dream   I drink wine stolen
from Jefferson's cellar. Break

bottles   burgundy torrents in
Monticello   my face submerged   mouth
wide   perch in lavish schools.

In the dream   I fulfill the dream.
Forget the plastic masks tangling
cedars   beaching on shore with the tide   moon

seemingly veiled with them.
We recognized you first.
I wanted the dream you professed.

Frescos without men
but leaves   wheat   mountain ranges.
In the dream   the war I fight is religious.

I'm mad. Jefferson reads his Koran.
The bomb is the heart clicking
in its aluminum shell.

Melancholy Initiated

You have traced yourself   moments
memorized until those moments

are rendered perpetual. You no longer
live the present. Time   merely review.

The willows whimper in loose chords
as wind has its way.

What has been discovered?
What bitterness has been devoured   made

into something where silence is solution?
It is at a different café where you drink

orange juice. The awning   some version
of taupe flaps as pollen makes you sneeze.

Crystal day yet fog is a rope tied around you.
What can be done with language indecipherable?

What is the purpose of morality
when that existence initiates dismay?

You are boxing in a ring yet your opponent
is unseen. There   in the capital   you've been

knocked down as the bleachered crowd cheers.
Let the bees feed on rosemary.

You taste their honey before it
is made   before what you see glows.

Storks to Ouarzazate

The wingspan of storks   like those airplanes

going somewhere. Landing somewhere

but we only see their undersides   the power

they evoke. The power Icarus defiled   his

legs covered in wax. At the airport

a girl with a pacifier in mouth   points a plastic

gun at her father. He smiles before pretending

to die   hand to chest   a gerbera blooming

through pallid cotton. Eyes closed   he sees

storks above. Such grace in what he perceives

as brawny beasts perhaps silly on ground   clumsy

on land where we are wedged.

How can love exist when all is unbalanced?

Landing in a country colonized   he

speaks the language of colony.

He questions this near seas   their darkening

through depth   time   his daughter's face.

She runs to him in black pumps but her

feet are too small for them. They click   slip

in mid-step. She doesn't fall.

The Beggars

It is the street. Those who inhabit

sidewalks   roads   the thinness of bough

like arms that don't match the heft of trees

pruned since wars' false end. That pillage

within us yet we walk invincibly among

heat   among beggars who are truth   ours.

Give me something I don't have.

Give me something I don't know I have.

That Which Began in Spring: A Banksy in Bethlehem

Squint as there is too much to see   too much
in front of us. That distance between their threat   ours.

But we will no longer choose blindness.
What we know is a truth wild

beneath ground   molten among
a labyrinth of veins.

Our veins   worn to paper.
This will cease.

Handkerchiefs over noses   mouths
to breathe.

Molotovs as bouquets of poppy   daffodil   jasmine
to toss at tanks   men with weapons

willing to wound.
They have wounded.

Men   boys in my country   murdered
yet the murderers live   roam

among us.
We let them   again   again.

A friend   his father in Bethlehem
are against a wall. Looking away

from a wall painted patiently,
Painted in Bethlehem

to say:
We will continue.

A friend   his father in Bethlehem
mimic with roses   red they will

toss at the graves
of those slain in

                                        Tunis
                                        Cairo

Gaza
Sanford

                                        Ferguson
                                        Tompkinsville.

We   squint.

$$\frac{46}{47}$$

We feed each other   pretend/
rosewater is common.

Blue Hijab

What becomes of a girl in blue hues?
Through a field   green where boulders

are serrated   ready to tumble   tear
earth exposing the clay

of a civilization
forced under.

This is where we feed.
Where sheep sully grass.

Where the shepherd sleeps
until his flock is fat.

The girl gathers vegetables   wild parsley.
At the market   she is accosted by a boy

dazzled by her blue hijab.
How each thread extends light.

That same light crushing over
his teeth in a mouth cascading.

A cement truck churns on her road home.
This is the mind attempting

something it hasn't. Thoughts more like
wire tangles   tricks in knots   traps

what shouldn't be trapped   loose
paper   plastic   this is how we are clogged.

We are weighed   distracted
rendered without progress.

How the telephone poles look more
like something left from a visit

undocumented. A phenomenon
unspoken of if only to maintain credibility.

Here internal lives are never exposed.
Pretending is not optional   not here where

we build   close ourselves in stone.
The onions make her cry as a caterpillar

crosses the counter of chipped tile.
What becomes of a girl in blue hues?

Her hijab on the floor   the potatoes
in the sink soaking   the dirt

disconnecting   assembling itself into
something with order   a sea floor shifting.

Christmas Alone in Morocco

Say all plans have failed.
The camping you'd hoped   the cedars
cut from jade   how sunlight plays with
itself but you don't see this.

It snows. On this day it snows in Africa.
Hum Hathaway in the taxi to Fes. The radio
raucous in a house your mother has
over decorated   such longing.

The three bowls you buy look
like snow   white   the blue you
don't see but know is there
because it is that which it reflects.

Cold that whips about when
you have been disappointed   when
you are made ancillary yet until then
imperative. The crises we learn

when everything must happen
in the way we imagine   precisely
that way   in the way we feel.
But no   left bewildered   pondering

the meaning of yourself   your
own ability to decipher those who
are now specter. You are specter.
How can this be?

Lunar

Decide not to witness
with the group.
Decide a dusty road.
Decide red sneakers   they
are most comfortable.

Boulders derived from
volcanoes block a street
but climb them anyway.
You will learn a language
from friends who tend

to the rotisserie   skins
of chickens drip   crisp.
Laugh at nothing
reasonable but think
of a sphere high. Think

of your arms almost liquid
stretching to a city you
love   around someone you
love in a city which doesn't glint.
The moon full   the blackening

of it with such haste.
The waist you feel
with slack arms
not any closer. What spills
over land at night?

Dew in the morning
but at night what happens?
What gives itself fully   sustains
us when we plea for depletion?
Moonlight through closed

curtains doesn't soothe.
The bed in shadows
resembling briar   this
horrible blue.
The moon higher   moonshine

drenched night where wild dogs
howl in packs.
The moon   so high.
So high the howl   the howl
of dogs at night.

The howl of illicit
drunks among scuffed
walls   the walls
that breathe   the mice
in those walls that wish to howl.

Decide your friends
are wrong when
they say there
is no ellipse   *not here.*
Why here?

Decide a woman
watches among spruce.
Decide what she sees
is sadistic   a veil flung
when somebody locks a door.

Muharram 1432

Clothes were being folded warm
against fingers   dry as autumn.

The bed will be made last.
It is the New Year.

Sunlight more like glass cuts skin.
Lament what has past   the previous

day where we stood in blue   wool
spun from sky   slate below soles   slick.

The sound of sea is sudden in ears.
If we'd waited there   if our conversation

had grown to cat's claw   I would
have stayed in its coil   loved

its coil tight   itchy.
But now there is a city of cedar

separating us.
Sitting in a café

your friends ask
me about you.

Gray day.
This new day   this froth

in a white cup   this crashing
against earth loose.

I have lost.
In this city where celebration

is locked in houses   I'm seen
openly   publicly silent drinking

from stained porcelain.
The walk home   more a vision.

Everyone else hovers above
ground as I'm yanked to clay.

Recite

But I thought this was love.
The beginning   ending   the sycamores' first leaves.

The becoming of someone else   more at ease   accepting
the world as itself   no protest.

Walks in the dark where dogs howl   the foam on the mouth
falling to gravel   a vein of it exposed   rapture.

The truth I know isn't so. Tell me why.
Explain my foolishness   the catalpa air we breathe.

Speak to that God who calls five times. Wash your face.
What does he say? Recite it all to me then go away.

Go to your part of town where asphalt grinds to dirt   where
owls nest in attics   those rooms where onions once dried.

Go to that place where independence was fought for   where
humiliation lives below tissue   fibrous   alive.

We are young among the old.
Mature among friends.

We will no longer share this world.

Settlement

There is Arabic beneath the sycamores.
From the market one man holds a watercolor
of a forest. Autumn then   leaves almost flame.
What happens when we are forced to give up?
When we destroy the interior   asbestos   metal

rods   plaster in jagged sheets?
When the sun shines on this
with more grace than the
days we waged protection?
When our faces were cut   red fell in flags.

A friend sells plums in Place Saint-Bruno.
Some are gold   most deep violet   glands
distilling infection to juice. He feels the weight
of shadow   the church   his mother
in the apartment obsessed with sparrows.

The women are naked here.
They see devotion both sinister   archaic.
I am a bomb in a dirty bed   in
a town that swallows itself.
These women visit me in

this bed when they are cold.
When their husbands don't see them   when
they come home drunk   bottles
breaking in hands. In the kitchen   I
keep pistachio pastries doused in honey.

We feed each other   pretend
rosewater is common. We breathe
anise   cardamom. That room   a medina.
Me as a boy   walking on stone   this warren
narrow   confusing   no one finds me.

There is Arabic beneath
the sycamores. We see rock
walls tumble but
speak nothing of this.
We survive humiliation.

The crumbling   the speed
of detached pieces
hurling in gunpowder.
There are cells in the debris   wet
attempting to remain wet.

The Red in Mountains

Poppies in the Middle Atlas are more
like flames individually contained   rendered

harmless now. Like dots on a canvas wild
with reeds   salvia dried for years.

These radiant petals are fragile yet closer
there is conflict. Skin torn from muscle   cut arteries

gushing   saturated mud. The elasticity of joints wet
without mystery. This quiet growth beneath sky

at the rim of aftermath. These battalions won't
cease their plights. Without limbs they continue

tearing away skin
with teeth   lipless   gums raw.

Snapping muscles to bouquets
that drip   fall about a mouth limp

yet still alive. In a café close   a man
drinks strawberries pulverized to juice.

A woman leaves poppies
on his table because she dreamed

of space   the pluming ground missiles make.
The ringing always remains.

The man thinks of his father.
His boutonniere   a sore forever spilling.

The Desert Unrequited

I want to talk about the desert.
How your eyelashes remind me
of the shapes made in sky.
The sight more shrill than
serene   wind cold cotton.
The clicking of metal   palms
chafed from hides beaten warm.

I want to talk about the desert.
Desolation so misconceived.
We are barefoot while climbing a dune.
Toes sifting sand too hot to linger.
We slip often. Backward   a concept
by which we internalize civilization.
Green suffocates to taupe.

I want to talk about the desert.
The orange bus that blends.
It is far from us. We wonder where it
will go. If it will go anywhere   pulled
still by heat winding. Earth more like
sugar   engine milled to steel flecks.

I want to talk about the desert.
The poisonous shrub that could
be collards but not. This peculiar
green out of time   loose in a glass
made to construe hours. Nothing
stewed   salted   the wing
of a turkey tender with vinegar.

I want to talk about the desert.
How your eyelashes remind me
of love you don't feel
or is somewhere else.
If it lived in irises   silence
would hold us hot. Clouds
would stretch then curl black.

Night Song in Tamazight

There is the voice that happens
among dark trees   among street
lights unlit. Among locusts hidden
in dead grass calling each other.
Their existence carried out through sound.

An insinuated voice splinters
the setting of sky.
Something written   adhered
to for survival. Survival here
among things wild.

Things made to seem wild.
A dog gasps yet finds a way to bark
as dark trees fold into themselves.
There is something secretive here.
Secretive in that voice's stability.

From a rotting house a boy plays
an instrument made in mountains.
Amplified electronically as wind forces
itself on faces   pushes grit in faces   forces
lavender in faces.

It pushes through shrubs   short
thorny but purple flowers are soft.
The boy is joined by others.
Their instruments pronounce
journey   settlement   the presence of hips.

Hair like fire writhes
in air   creates currents.
Someone has left.
A woman has left.
He wants to see her.

He wants to see his love
not the road she walked   the dirt
her feet flung into air.
Her perfume is air.
He sings:

The dust   the road I breathe.
My love I breathe. The night
I breathe my love. The fire
doesn't burn yet it makes
things fall. My life falls like walls.

The voice has no tin
yet the instruments do.
There is purity in the weight
it creates. The heft on shoulders
unlike wheat   unlike stones

this weight is welcomed.
This weight makes us stop.
We don't worry about the moon
waning   the kingdom
in sudden combustion.

We are in a place where sight
opens to another. Where dark
trees are hands pulling night   pulling
wind for the voice to call   for a boy
to play   pushing a woman to flee.

African America

He is writing in a journal.
The café where tea is cheap   green.
A fountain is close. He laments a woman
who loves him. This is what she says in letters   over

the telephone   in songs she records   sends
in beaten brown boxes.
Two dark men stare   walk pass his table.
Wicker more like wire   tarnished

silver woven into something more than utilitarian.
He looks up   *Salaam.* Shakes their
wet hands   *Mauritania   Sudan?*
America   he says.

One man removes his shades mirroring
the mildew of roof   *Ah   African America.*
The sun is a marigold as they leave.
Black shoes to paved road echoing familiarity.

A boy on Lenox tapping for change.   A father
leaving the house   the porch   the driveway   the street.
The horn of the Thunderbird is a call
to the God he used to love.

South

What is there to say of disaster?
The aftermath   eerie   the land
clumped   ravaged. But that fired
ground has brought crocuses.

You have purchased almonds
from a man heading south.
He seemed weary folding them in paper.
What has been drained from him?

What are you drained of walking among
dogs whose ribs are defined through skin.
Where do your crocuses grow?
The blossoms like starfish

on saturated sand as a satellite
glows   such sumptuousness.
South to sacrifice something alive.
You are your father's only son.

The man who sold almonds is the same.
You have met on a day draining
itself into something you can't
understand   can't articulate but

the dogs know as they leave you.
As you think of the man who
sold you almonds.
What will he see in the south?

At the Eastern Market: Asiatic Lilies

It was the smell. That squally perfume
somehow sonic. A closed hand opening
holding dust   glucose as gloss.
She turns away from hostas   phlox

to inspect those tall lilies   the pink
within them like some beautiful rash
that would disappear by morning.
The market   cleaner than you remembered.

The giant rooster painted on entrance not as
perturbed   violent   brutish eyes not as bugged.
Allergic to lilies yet in love with their scent.
This is an old conundrum.

The unfairness   what we are given
more than once. That place where we linger
for too long. Where we give up almost
everything   rendered senseless.

But today we load them into the trunk.
You are dizzy   Ornette Coleman fills the brain
as if filling that room in Tangier where
a mad man pretended not to be mad.

On the road back   a man hits a woman
in a wheelchair   fist to shoulder   nose.
Perhaps her lover for years   all she has.
Question distance   how far

that perfume propels   why you have left.
Those left befuddled   turquoise
strings of it throttling. They are getting
older   mortality abruptly grave.

We need you   they say.
You are not only you   such bewilderment.
A severing of a space you guarded   planned.
The world is quickly crowded.

We are taken in wheelbarrows.

Collapse

1.

As if in a blast   a rocket
taking off from some deserted place.
Smoke   fire of some rare fuel once bison   a herd

frozen   buried   baked   beetle   worm eaten   digested.
This is why we war.
Why towers glint   seem to grow in sand.

But there isn't a blast   merely a bus on the verge of dilapidation.
But some parts of the engine are new. The strangeness
of shimmering steel   a few pipes of it oiled among the corroded.

2.

We meet beneath sycamores whose leaves
seem to burn   twitch from branches brittle.
The moon   porous as skin.

How it beams as if a god   an eye of a god going blind.
Who will guide him after he has guided so many
waging a kind of stability?

But we walk inside the bus closing our eyes
to that larger eye losing itself.
Houses half built whose roofs are arrows dipped in wax.

Perhaps made this way to protect stars at which they are aimed.
At a man's command   they'd thrust into sky.
People perpetually facing the sky.

Necks slowly wrapped in iron   a reassured
kingdom on a continent where mines
erupt randomly.

Placed there by groups myopic   sick
with false power   a colonial period
when resources were locked in bone boxes.

3.

How the bus shakes.
In   out of sleep   dream.
The rain   the sound of seeds spilling.

Squash seeds over land that will bloom orange
for women to pick   stuff with raisins   cumin   cinnamon   pepper
salted rice then stewed.

Blossoms on round tables   in wide
baskets   affix behind ears   place
in green soda bottles.

The sun itself in that night.
The brightness of dream unlike day   such clarity
when eyes are imagined   the world

imagined   seen in cellulous piles   in pollen   in food
eaten slowly. The blooming within the mouth   spheres
leaving the mouth   glowing spheres wet with saliva   dry

mica illuminating as if part of a giant chandelier   the interior
of lungs as glass   copper wire holding everything together.
We breathe.

4.

The sputter of wheels between consciousness   unconsciousness.
Blue through windows thick as oracle   dark.
How it passes over faces in cubes. Stacks on faces making them

seem sealed with mortar   made by hands   rough   dirty   skilled
in only that making. Your father   our fathers creating us from clod.
Our awareness elsewhere or perhaps none at all.

Rhythmic road down a mountain
where oaks arc as if afraid of sky.
Dark sky.

Dark oaks.
Night itself.
The night where our eyes back   forth in sockets widening.

5.

It is a town listless until the bus stops.
Bull cadavers swinging from chains.
A man fans charcoal beneath a grill.

Like the bars of a prison cell yet hot   meant
to sear   darken flesh in lines to eat   wound   punishment
for life. They are eating meat sandwiches.

Beef   day old bread with salt   cumin.
A snack for the dream   energy for the dreaming left.
But you stand away from them.

Watch a truck of chickens stop.
The driver smokes a cigarette   blows a tunnel into air.
A tunnel where a crowd is martyred.

A crowd in a capital loud   young   poor   flattened
by bullets   officers with clubs   the wailing they only hear.
The wailing of women in villages where they were born.

The wailing when they left.
The wailing they will commence
when they know what they have done   whom they have followed.   74

The chickens on their way to slaughter.
You eat a pear understanding something you will not reveal.
The smell of diesel   chickens resting in filth.

This is a scene somehow traditional.
Those taken on a truck to a place unknown by those carried.
Exhaust leaving the muffler as if collectively saying   *we give up.*

We are satisfied with the life we've led.
Prepare for what will be grueling.
The torture is certain.

Stars.
A few through drizzling sky.
The sky as an iron sieve   fine yet corroded.

6.

It is the south where the earth goes coral.
That change from umber north   as if salmon
decided suicide. Their leaping   flapping

about that barren place   their remains
a peculiar beauty. How generosity can do this.
The self sacrificed for others   most of whom unborn.

Perhaps their memory of desert once ocean brought
them back. The spawning   their origins
distant   reclaiming is pinnacle.

You are startled in that dawn   in that coral
dawn   that coral earth of departed lives.
We stop.

The bus stops.
We have tea   tawny   sweet in glasses where
mint leaves float as if the pads of lilies.

Ash trees spill over walls.
You stare at their contrasting colors.
Leaves as fingers tearing the pink walls down.

The quiet there   no longer.
Your voice through telephone wire to a woman
near water   drinking water   swimming

in water slightly tainted with algae.
Cells splitting as
the sun warms.

You are disappointed?
You miss me?
You are swimming to drown memory?

Memory of me drinking water near you?
Swimming near you?
My watery hands?

7.

Palms that look like pineapples.
A pool with a turquoise floor we
can see without difficulty.

Stone steps lead to the floor   semiprecious.
You tie a blue scarf around your neck   the sea
around your neck   the sky around your neck.

You are this earth. Perhaps ruined earth
as it always is. As long as we are here
ruining it   it is ruined.

What can we do with ruins?
Destroy?
Rebuild?

Civilizations pose
questions   answer
questions in wild thrusts.

8.

Rest on the green bench beneath
the date palm. The brown fronds
will eventually break away.

Someone will make them
into a roof which will collapse.
You will collapse when someone leaves.

Leave me. I won't fall.

I won't fall for you.

But if my joints give   I will wait

until you leave. Use something

else to sustain height.

Loving the floor is private.

You will not see this.

9.

We are mud as are our houses.
Flat as sky   brown   coral.
You have removed your jacket.

You sit in a place meant for such as you
put on a wide straw hat.
Coral earth   then green palms.

They produce a fruit where their
sugar enters the blood directly.
After fasting   this is eaten first.

You are cobalt   cerulean   royal.
Brown face shielded from
a hot star as if gathering

tobacco in Virginia.
From the window   Jefferson
stares at his son.

10.

Call this land yours. Speak languages
native   colonial.
There are sequins on the saffron wall.

Count

all

of

them

to

find

your-

self.

11.

Here women wear veils even though
roads are shadow.
Billowing veils into circles   tubes.

Are these women djinns?
Scorching wind beneath cotton with onyx eyes.
We are supposed to look away but we don't.

Street lights curve above them yet no luminescence.
It is morning or early afternoon.
Dust ribbons around them.

12.

The dunes are like mountains but feet aren't stable.
Smooth   peaked   burnt buttercream but there is poison.
The shock of it green   fibrous.

Green is supposed to be life but here it is not.
This is the first time.
That scarf around your neck means south.

A man paints your face blue   calls you brother.
You are closer to blue   Amazigh blue   Tuareg blue   Arab
blue in Africa.

                                        This is a meeting of blue.

                                        A tune played on banjo.

13.

Blue tied about the head before climbing on camelback.
These animals are giants in a perpetual desert.
Their eyelashes copper in light.

You are guided by desert men.
They are sand   blood you can't see.
What beats in them echoes through desolation.

We hear it as the camels slope   as dunes recede   as we
become shadow on sand waves modulating.
The first to ride a camel was perhaps insane.

Perhaps lost his life quickly.
Or did that camel bow   give away its back
to a desperate man   a man seeking water

with wheat in his hands? The shadows wider.
Did he see those salmon dying? Schools of them
on brown sand submitting their coral?

14.

Cover your nose   face.
Face that which attacks or loves.
Blue is your new skin.

What you wear among sand   the group
you are with but not.
Your feet leave holes that someone

must fill   a universe must fill if it is to evolve.
Evolve for us.
This is truth.

We are necessary to sustain this idea.
We are paltry without this   the world
from the perspective of beasts.

15.

This weight.

This person divineless.

This sand sears hooves sinking.

Being gentle is practiced.

Something conscious for it can be replaced

by something else   the opposite.

But we agree to be gentle to each other.

The prophet has told us this.

The journey itself contract.

Silver salmon hide their coral insides.

We dream of them flinging about our legs.

We eat some of them   leave others to dye sand.

16.

It is near the mosque.
The square where people play or think
of playing   where one man gives coins to beggars.

Cloaked in pale wool   blue
crowns embroidered
at the neck.

He doesn't shine.
He is more like dawn.
The breaking of something old.

He notices your blue face.
The others you've come with
are invisible to him even though

they change space   make
it heavy in a village where
the ruling family

began their rule.
Where they asked people to follow them.
Where they talked about the prophet.

Convert me to someone I wish I were.
Convert me to water in desert.
I am a beggar but I don't want coins.

He is Bedouin.
His sons look like you but taller   turbaned.
What tribe are you?

From where of this land have you come?

17.

Dark men in white play percussion   sing percussive.

This is the south.

You are southern   always southern

even though born in the north.

This is your rhythm.

The trance you are besieged.

The winding of neck   the currents

in arteries   this is who you are.

18.

There is the promise to turn.

The logical reaction to a familiar voice   one

inaudible for months.

The raucousness of a city gone gray.

Its wild factories smelting earth.

But there is caution. The danger of being judged

for the absence you chose.

Wind without spearmint.

You avoid the glance.

The world it would grow   leafless willows   houses

without roofs   a cyclone of scorpions grieving.

The shemagh around your neck is tight.

The desert at night   you were a mountain

child in a classroom without heat.

Cold when taking physics   calculus exams.

I throw tangerines into the Atlantic.

My voice sinks in its crests.

19.

They are bargaining for peppers.
Have arrived on bikes   feet.
You notice a truck being emptied by a boy.

His wheelbarrow filling with cow heads.
Their teeth clamping tongues gone taut.
You hear them humming.

Their hairless faces blotchy.
What is the punishment for decapitation?
Does the boy know?

Does he see what he throws
into the blue wheelbarrow?
The humming again.

Brown hands pushing the wheelbarrow
but it is not being rolled to a cemetery.
The humming again.

In another city   the heads are human.
The aftermath of revolt.
The secrets a country keeps.

The secrets we keep from ourselves
when we beam in a place where we
are asked to be dim.

We march.
We are observed.
We are taken in wheelbarrows.

20.

You buy tangerines.

There are collards   okra here in baskets.

We are brown in a coral south.

The air is breath   the buildings on the verge of crumb.

A herd of donkeys eat plastic strewn in a lot

as if seeds but nothing grows there.

Two girls stare at the minaret.

Their hands cover their mouths.

21.

Follow me outside the village   outside dream where the bus waits.

The tires over meteors like broken black marbles.

There is water for you to wash your face   clear water swirls to blue.

The desert has given up here.

But you hear the sea suddenly.

Whirl

Whirl   whirl red dust.

Whirl tall to sky less than cobalt.
Whirl into funnels   layers of air.
Among houses white with sun   whirl.
As if Sufi   whirl.
Whirl a world wrecked.

A trance   no land   no country   whirl.
Whirl to towers loose.
The next wonder   the coming   whirl.
Whirl even if speculative.
Whirl with might   maybe.

Whirl   whirl the dust red.

Whirl it all round.
Wonder wildly whirl.
Whirl wicked whimsy.
Whirl the black sheep to a black field.
Whirl a vision fired yet clear.

Whirl with me.
Whirl debris green.
Wind a howl   whirl.
Whirl dissipation.
Whirl it all atomless.

Whirl   whirl red dust.

Two Parakeets in Temara

They were in a cage on the floor.
Sunlight through the kitchen window
in a crescent. You are told their singing
isn't beautiful. In fact   no songs
at all   racket   tuneless   two blind
roosters whose sky is forever breaking.

Omar lifts the cage.
One bird reminds him
of celery   the garden
behind his mother's house   her
tearing its leaves on the counter   the poplars
of his village in the mountains.

There has always been envy.
The humming of giant
cars   their sheen
along streets where buildings
are a series of blocks   angles
rubbed to rip heart to ribbons.

Desire dissolves but
it is always there.
When the blood dries
it is in crystals.
The capital makes
these more copious.

The blue parakeet is a stream where
he raced   won the gazes of girls
who seemed more ice than anything else.
The story water tells as it shimmers.
How blue feathers liquefy   the fat
of the mind oily with ideas.

These we often leave for waste.
Why should we bother forms
seemingly benign?
Danger is often hidden.
The bang that blasts
without preconception.

Omar is gentle with
the parakeets like
something in tissue
which when wrapped
began almost in particles.
He hardly holds them.

They feel the faint
mazes of fingers.
He wishes they'd sing
something in Arabic.
Something that would
summon a congregation

of believers in something
more than religion.
Something more attainable   in more
demand than a life after itself.
Something that would mend
everything he has torn.

Time

But this is for a time.
A time that slides down branches.
A time seen in mirrors as a trapezoid
of light in constant tremor.
A time when wind is cold   rain colder.
The car has stopped in a town where
sheep   bull heads are eaten.
A time when we stop for breakfast   the coffee
some version of mud.
A time to return to mountains even though
dangerous   even though south was the destination.
A time to prepare for death.
The way the streets run red
but you pretend rust.
A time to mourn love imagined.
Your love for me imagined.
Its reality   currents in air.
A time made complicated
by bombs   the coming
bombs   those eventually
rendering us missing.
A time to perhaps be alone   to be
safe among walls   ceilings that leak.
A time that slides down skin.

Sewing Mars

The poppies in her hands were stolen
but she didn't know it. The field more
abandoned than possessed. She needs
them for a mattress   a red stuffing

that will stain muslin. Spheres of it
like some planet where water is found
yet no life   none we can detect   understand.
Stems on the floor   green rods

will brown   blow away when shutters
are wide   when wind is itself   wild   wanderlust.
But that room will remain a place
of slumber   intoxicating without

matches   smoke.
She is fastidious   needle   silk
thread tightening seams.
She isn't phased when the men

arrive soiled   rank.
When they stare   her
face sunburned
yet translucent.

She has traveled. The flush of her
from some dead star. Philosophy   yes.
We bleed where we sleep   where we rest.
The mind letting go of itself   cloth

absorbing its perfume   its sweet terror.
She will not scream even though we are evil.
Up from clay   our lives.
The pulling   pushing of it   no reaction.

The tea kettle boils over.
Red liquid   acrid   shockingly so.
Green leaves brown with heat.
She continues to sew that mattress

of poppy   mattress of Mars.
The shutters blow wide
as the men leave. In the sky   egrets
white as Calacatta.

Stillness

The strangeness of brake lights on a road
seemingly deserted. The tail of car   garnets
tersely luminous   an idea that flashes
just before the call meant to stop you.
Meant to bring you to that hard

ground   knees   forehead bruised
brilliantly but you keep walking.
See a blue window   blue light
from a window as blue as your face   as blue
as the song you heard during dinner

where fennel   zucchini were
seared with cumin   where rice was
a surprise   sticky stout grains. But the two
you ate with didn't see you. Didn't
hear your spoon against the bowl. Didn't

smell the soot in your hair. You were alone
in that room as you are on that road.
The call between temples   ears as you
speak to yourself: *regret   regret.*
Regret that lost day   that day when

no one sees you   not even you. Not even
the one who passes. The one to whom you
speak only to hear yourself. The one who
blends into night. That window   tiny   a blue
square on a second floor. She sees the same

but to her it is the sea spilling from
that window   the sea of her childhood
in the south. Her father's hand
on the window facing the sea.
But you hear the sea suddenly.

Waves wrangling rocks.
Waves foaming against feet.
What have you become?
Is this some wish to leave?
Mountains too high   finally too

high   too close to space but don't
you love space? The space you saw
through telescope too frightening now?
You are away from revolt. Away from
cities where martyrs are too willing.

Will me a cloak of charged dust.
Will me this kind of visibility   strange
visibility   visibility where only
pieces are visible   the cloak alluring.
Will this to me now among strange

houses
constantly
being
built
    destroyed.

Pondering A

It is the absence. The tiles wearing

variably on a street we paced.

What is this agony where shadow becomes

paper doors one tears only to find another?

What the mind creates when it longs.

When someone old struggles with a crate

of grapefruits where stems   leaves jut

in bayonets   through flesh   air like flesh

of parrots   stringy   tough but mine is not.

Like Saint Sebastian in a field where fig leaves

are comfort yet susceptible to an inherited anarchy.

Reinventing art   one piece of art   its

combat feral. This lushness is some nightmare

which has beauty   moments of quietude

when we ponder the glory of land.

How can this be as we float   merge

with ether then land? Forgetting is as impossible

as not breathing   but let me be.

Let me be here inside this absence   inside

this misery without escape.

We Sell Watermelons All Night Long

We are aware beneath tarp canopies.
The way they billow as if signaling departure
but we are here all night long   twenty-four
hours a day. Praising the event of knife

through rind as if opening a planet or that
which is inside us all   a gush of water
where rafts are epidemic.
Wedges for free   temptation from vine

that spirals   that is meant to die   to fold
into the meat of earth. This time of unbearable
heat relieved by green boulders we sell with
the promise to drench   everything red.

This not after the desert   not after ballooning blue
atop camels but just during summer's boil   a day
hammering something into place   after reclining
on a bed because it is most sensible. They come

to us barrel-armed as if preparing to hold
a chubby child who is most loved.
This is love. The love
of season pure. Neruda's love   the sweetness

of hidden water   thirst defeated.
Earth smudged trousers   earth under nails
is the uniform of chant   the grace of toil.
The seeds we sowed on a peninsula we

haven't forgotten but our land is where
we have landed   where we should be   where
we continue to plant. These weekend
markets when our truck is full   we sell.

An Amphibian Questions in a Locker Room

Waiting for water to warm.
A man stands beneath the shower   soap
pollutes in crests yet smells of fenugreek.

I pretend to be part of the drain.
The stain of bronze   an age where
busts populated a kingdom sold away.

I wonder if he notices my attempted stillness.
The blob of blubber   the beaks I escaped.
Will I escape him?

The scrubbing he does after weights   running.
The salt   oil   skin flooding tiles.
He will be stronger after sleep but not me.

Crawling through a pipe or leaping
in a room when the floor cools.
Hiding if others appear wild or at all.

Will he attack just because I am here?
Not outside   not where
he supposes I should be?

If I were there   he'd still question
my place in grass   water
yet my blood is cold?

He sees me with soap in his eyes.
Our eyes are in each other's.
I'm wishing for gnats.

In fact   I'm seeing
them everywhere.
This is a swamp.

I am afraid of him.
He isn't afraid of me
or he's apathetic

or he aches   just wants to leave
the shower   the dull room where
mold is bleached from ceiling.

Peculiar drain.
The stain I resemble with pulse.
There is no need for escape   not yet.

To Guide in Agadir

We are surrounded. Stopped by a crowd   prayer
mats slung over shoulders.
There is conversation   the beaches   the weekend
market for lemons   milk.

A crippled man has fallen. Is pulled up
by men in jellabas   younger.
Their mats tossed to gravel   to
that side of road avoided.

A ruler refuses renouncement even though
bombs crater. We understand delusion
in secret   in cold rooms where storm-petrels are audible.
The morning   a sliced pear   bread where honey webs.

This is how we live.
Blasts in chests without visibility.
A village where sheep lick
shepherds to nasturtiums.

Who guides whom to slaughter?

Apart

Medusa doesn't die in water.
It is the sky that takes her apart.

Pulls her slowly to pieces   poison
in streaks   long   white.

Who is so cruel to the cruelest?
So blue   all to bed   all sick   unrequited

everything   everything violent.
Gone   we are.

July Street

Ahmed walks with his sister on July Street
searching for shoes   beige leather   something on July Street.

Plastic strings of light   the strange flashing   the aggression
of merchants   their titanic insistence on July Street.

This day is supposed to be celebratory   sadness
for another time yet there must be cynics on July Street.

A djinn combs his hair while looking at Ahmed
but doesn't understand his solace on July Street.

His lips are smoke   the rest of him fire;
he wants to drop serpents on July Street.

The hijab his sister wears won't protect from such
cold coils; she sees a woman in sequins on July Street.

Her brother hears yelling   hears their father waking
famished even though meat sizzles on July Street.

The store they enter is filled with ferocious men;
shoes shine phosphorescently   the djinn is dazzled on July Street.

The girl holds her brother's arm as she ponders shoes   as she
notices sequin littered sidewalks on July Street.

Are there other women who love discs   adornments with sparkle;
who love to hold eyes in horn boxes   no surrender on July Street?

The djinn will cover himself in sequins only
to get the girl interested   to mimic the sacred on July Street.

Ahmed doesn't understand his sister's gaze   her attention
to simplicity unlike the crash of cymbals on July Street.

Percussive soles: wood   leather   rubber   they
walk in curious symmetry on July Street.

Their father dreams of his tongue elongated   lapping
a candied floor the djinn creates; this dream isn't eccentric on July Street.

They walk to a temporary home   a hotel room
that is dead or waits for such a signal on July Street.

Ahmed knows Myronn but doesn't understand why he
writes this poem; this enigma won't be solved on July Street.

Mercy

Pretend not to love.
Pretend air sustains nothing.
Pretend because it is easy.

Easy to be among elms at night.
To walk among elms at night   their
shadows fortresses bending to labyrinth.

There your breath as mist
strangely sudden   strangely waterlogged.
Breath as a bouquet you carry

to the one you love but pretend not to.
Pretend because you are weak   been
weakened by a past oddly free.

By a past where your glow   that glow
rendered others blind   love luminous.
Those blinded mocked in dark glasses.

Mocked without hesitation at your lack
of hesitation. *This is whom I love. This one.*
This love is mine even if it isn't. Hear me.

You let them drag you through town.
Clothes ripped by rocks.
Who knew the blind were vicious?

So bruised you have remained.
Wounds like storms on Jupiter
forever hostile. But this hostility

is inside that which you deny.
Sky of latticed lightning   wind
wild without wonder.

Notes

"Blue Hijab": A hijab is a head covering worn by Muslim women. It is suggested in the Koran that a woman may consider wearing such in order to maintain modesty.

"Silver": Younès Belhanda is an international Moroccan football player, born in France, who currently plays for the Ukrainian club Dynamo Kyir.

"What You've Been Given," "To Guide in Agadir": Jellabas are traditional Imazighen (the original peoples of North Africa) articles of clothing which are loose fitting, long tunics, worn by both men and women. They are usually made of wool.

"To Guide in Agadir": The "ruler" referenced is Muammar el-Quaddafi.

"The Treachery of Dream": On February 17, 2012, FBI officials arrested Amine El Khalifi, a twenty-nine-year-old Moroccan man who attempted a suicide bomb attack on the U.S. Capitol Building. He had lived in the U.S. since he was sixteen, entering the country with a visitor's visa. The visa had been expired for years and he was living illegally in Virginia.

"Collapse," "July Street": Djinns are mentioned in the Koran and in ancient Arabian tales as beings/spirits who are capable of influencing human kind by changing into various forms.

"Muharram 1432": Muharram is the first month of the Islamic calendar.

"Honor": Amina Filali was a sixteen-year-old girl who committed suicide by ingesting rat poisoning, after being forced to marry the man who raped her. Article 475 is a Moroccan penal code which allows a rapist, specifically of a minor, to marry his victim instead of being prosecuted and sentenced to prison time. This incident occurred in 2012.

"What We Survive": Place Saint-Bruno is a public square in Grenoble, France. The city itself has sizable North African communities.

Acknowledgments

Belleville Park Pages (Paris): "The Beggars," "Sheep: Flood Foreseen"

The Broome Street Review: "Muharram 1432," "Two Parakeets in Temara"

The Café Review: "Recite," "Time"

Callaloo: "Blue Hijab," "The Waiting," "South," "To Guide in Agadir," "Pondering A," "Stillness," "July Street," "Whirl," "As a Woman Collects Leaves," "African America," "Storks to Ouarzazate," "At the Eastern Market: Asiatic Lilies," "Treachery of Dream"

Callaloo ART: "Spring Moths"

CURA: A Literary Magazine of Art and Action: "Lacquer"

Eleven Eleven: "Consider the Dust," "Towers," "Melancholy Initiated"

Gargoyle: "Gigou," "The Desert Unrequited"

The Lumberyard: "Settlement"

The Offending Adam: "Beat," "What We Call Destroyed," "Haze," "Silver"

Prairie Schooner: "Mercy"

Puerto del Sol: "Kingdom"

Union Station Magazine: "The Red in Mountains," "Sewing Mars"

Zócalo Public Square: "What You've Been Given"

"Blue Cards in the Café of Old Men," "Sewing Mars," and "Night Song in Tamazight" were published in a chapbook including the winners of the 6th Annual Nazim Hikmet Poetry Prize.

photo credit: Saad Ben Elafdil

Myronn Hardy is the author of three previous books of poems: *Approaching the Center*, winner of the PEN/Oakland Josephine Miles Award, *The Headless Saints*, winner of the Hurston/Wright Legacy Award, and *Catastrophic Bliss*, winner of the Griot-Stadler Prize for Poetry. He has received fellowships from the Anneberg Foundation, Djerassi, the Bread Loaf Writers' Conference, the Sacatar Foundation, and Fundación Valparaiso. He divides his time between Morocco and New York City.

The Green Rose Prize

2014:   Kathleen Halme
        My Multiverse

2013:   Ralph Angel
        Your Moon

2012:   Jaswinder Bolina
        Phantom Camera

2011:   Corey Marks
        The Radio Tree

2010:   Seth Abramson
        Northerners

2009:   Malinda Markham
        Having Cut the Sparrow's Heart

2008:   Patty Seyburn
        Hilarity

2007:   Jon Pineda
        The Translator's Diary

2006:   Noah Eli Gordon
        A Fiddle Pulled from the Throat of a Sparrow

2005:   Joan Houlihan
        The Mending Worm

2004:   Hugh Seidman
        Somebody Stand Up and Sing

2003:   Christine Hume
        Alaskaphrenia
        Gretchen Mattox
        Buddha Box

2002:   Christopher Bursk
        Ovid at Fifteen